"The higher your energy level, the more efficient your body. The more efficient your body, the better you feel and the more you will use your talent to produce outstanding results."

TONY ROBBINS

CONTENTS

Introduction	1
Problem	3
Motivation	10
Happiness	12
The happiness diet	13
Take more brain herbs	21
Junk light consumption	21
Brain diet	24
Brain limiting foods	26
Energy	30
Sugar & fat	34
Exercise	36
A winner's diet	39
Fighting cravings	43
Work desk practical tips	46
Sleep	50
Epilogue	51

INTRODUCTION

To get the best possible results in the workplace you need to be the best version of yourself. You may notice that in the workplace, often referred to as a jungle, some people shine naturally and always win, whilst others seem to consistently lose. But how does one decide to shine too?

Good thing you asked, as that switch can help you work smarter, longer, sharper, strategically and even enable you to think clearer when communicating in the office. That switch, the unfair advantage, is choosing to live a healthier lifestyle. And this book will be your guide to fast track your health and ultimately fast track your career.

Firstly, I want to say congratulations for getting yourself a copy of this handbook, I know you will find it useful. A lot of people I encounter tend to sacrifice their health for their careers; and although this may appear to be a good strategy in the short term, long term they experience burnouts and eventually habitual burnouts. Which of course slows them down. However, with proper planning and information you can keep going, sort of like a Duracell battery that is solar-powered.

Once you use the concepts in this book, increase your productivity and secure that promotion be sure to email me at paul@dungubook.com

PROBLEM

Health is wealth - a phrase I often say. I say this because when a person is ill, the most prevalent thing on their mind is how to get well, not how much money they have. So, health is the true wealth; but it's common for us to sacrifice our health for wealth. When referring to health, I mean both physical and mental wellbeing. Both are crucial because the better you feel the better you do and if you're feeling better, you are capable of so much more.

As a child, I used to love going to McDonalds to get the ice cream and cone for 59p. I'd walk up to the counter, give the cashier the 60p and wait to receive my penny change. That penny always went into the spiral charity coin box.

And if you remember, once you put a penny in, it begins its downward course, rolling in an appealing motion until it gets to the very bottom going into complete abyss. This is the downward spiral. Towards the beginning of the decline the effects are not that noticeable but once the motion starts and picks up speed, one problem leads to another that leads to another and before you know it, you're taking time off work and experiencing potential ailments.

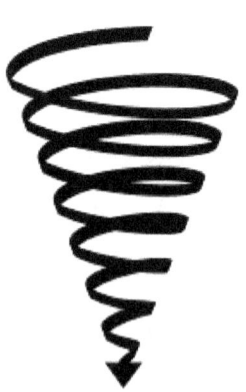

For example, there tend to be five archetypes of people in a corporate role. There is the workaholic, the alpha, the gossiper, the superhero and the slacker. It's also possible to have more than one archetype within us. The workaholic and alpha will do anything to succeed and get praise for the work they produced. In order to succeed, they may make health sacrifices, such as, lack of sleep or poor eating habits. By helping you develop healthy habits, this book will make you become a superhero, with secrets to supercharge yourself with superpowers from eating 'superfoods'.

Most employers offer wellness programs to their employees to help increase wellbeing in the workforce, to avoid the expensive costs of absenteeism and presenteeism.

Companies lose up to £1,600 per employee per year as a result of failing to effectively engage employees in wellness. This stems from presenteeism, a loss of workplace productivity resulting from employee health problems and/or personal issues and absenteeism. Absenteeism means being absent from work for several reasons, including ill health.

That's why it's in your employer's best interest to help encourage healthy living. Research shows that 60% of people in the workplace want to be healthier but the main reasons for not doing so are not having enough time, lack of motivation and not knowing what to do. This book aims to change that.

MOTIVATION

When starting a new journey, the burst of energy to start that journey is motivation. Motivation is the reason for people's actions, willingness and goals. How does one become motivated to live healthier and where does the motivation come from?

The first step, as cliché as it is, is to start with the why. I met a computer engineer who works 10hour days sat in front of a computer. After his shifts he heads home to his excited 8-year-old son and 5-year-old daughter.

However, after a long day at work, he is too tired and "not fit enough" to match their energy. He just wants to go to bed. One day, he gets home at the usual time to find the excitement has gone from his children's eyes, they have gotten so used to disappointment, they aren't excited anymore. It was at that moment he decided to change his life to be more energetic, lose weight and become healthier. That was his why. What is yours?

My why was purely physical, yours can be too. All my teenage years I was chubby, I adopted a slight forward lean when walking to hide my 'moobs' (man boobs). Until one day I had the light bulb moment that I want abs, a ludicrous thought but I was determined. I signed up for the gym that day and I worked my ass off for three and a half months straight. I lost 4.5 stone and achieved my goal. Think about your goal, your why and how can you use your why to ignite a burning desire to achieve the goal.

Take a moment and write down 5 things that would make you happier right now. As you are writing understand how you feel. Which of these 5 things carry the most feeling?

That is your why, use that why and get fired up about it. Visualise your exact goal. Think about it before you sleep and imagine it is already done; how you would look, how you would feel, how you would walk into the office in your shining new outfit. The feeling of throwing away your old baggy clothes... or burning them, as you've bought a whole new wardrobe. Embrace this feeling. That feeling is going to carry you when things get hard or temptation strikes. Temptation always strikes.

In this book, I'm going to give you the practical theory, but reality can be harder, the chocolate cake smell might block your senses and you need to be ready for it.

Motivation will help and so will knowledge. Just be ready because when you become the best you, you will excel in every single area of your life. You will exude confidence, you will speak with passion and your ideas will be appreciated. I hope by now you're getting fired up. Let's get started.

HAPPINESS

Every office has their highflyers. They have that magnetism and charisma that attracts opportunities to them. They seem to naturally be happy and achieve. The simple fact is that happiness increases productivity. The better you feel, the better you do and then you feel even better because you are doing better – that's the upwards spiral. The spiral you should be on.

Happiness can be influenced from outwards; your job, office but this book will focus on practical steps you can do yourself in order to radiate from the inside out.

THE HAPPINESS DIET

Through our daily routines, diet and habits we have the power to make ourselves happier. This is by adapting our routines and diets to impact the chemical balances in the brain. There are four primary chemicals (neurotransmitters) in the brain that affect happiness, these are dopamine, oxytocin, serotonin and endorphins.

Over the last decade, Science has evolved to allow neuroscientists to view the brain in detail and measure neural activity. This has helped give an increase in clues to the underlying factors that contribute to depression. One of the findings is that chronic stress causes low serotonin levels in the brain and low serotonin activity is linked with suicides, both attempted and successful.

So, what is serotonin? According to Psychology Today, serotonin is the "confidence molecule." They explain that ultimately the link between higher serotonin and a lack of rejection sensitivity allows people to put themselves in situations that will bolster self-esteem, increase the feelings of worthiness and create a sense of belonging.

This means that higher serotonin leads to increased confidence and doing things that challenge yourself, such as going outside your comfort zone, is one way to increase serotonin. Opt to do a talk at work, lead a workshop or put forward new ideas to management. These micro wins will increase serotonin levels and confidence as serotonin flows when you feel significant or important.

Another way to boost serotonin is by diet and lifestyle. The first thing I'll touch on is herbs. Herbs are plants with leaves, seeds, flowers used for flavouring, food, medicine or perfume. I have a whole book on herbs called Herb List Guide for Beginners and I am a practicing herbalist. There is a powerful herb that most people benefit from in low quantities but may not understand how they are benefiting. Eat a chocolate bar today, minus feeling sugar high, you may also feel a sense of happiness. That happiness is to do with the small percentage of cacao found in chocolate.

Cacao is the raw form of chocolate. Cacao itself contains serotonin and it also boosts the body's natural production of serotonin, increasing our mood and ability to fend off stress. You can get cacao powder and use it in your morning smoothie instead of coffee a few times a week. You will get a small boost in energy as Cacao contains both caffeine and theobromine, which are stimulants. With Cacao you won't get the same comedown as you would with coffee, it's more of a slow releasing energy boost. Other minerals essential in the production of serotonin are magnesium and tryptophan both high in Cacao.

There are other herbs in my collection that I use for brain health such as Lemongrass and Ginseng. The calming properties of Lemongrass make it very helpful in promoting a good night's sleep, especially where stress and anxiety are the cause of sleepless nights. It helps to soothe the mind and body by inducing the release of serotonin, the precursor to the sleep hormone melatonin.

The other hormone we'll discuss is dopamine. Dopamine, referred to as the reward hormone, motivates us to act toward goals, desires, and needs, and also gives a surge of reinforcing pleasure when achieving them. This hormone sparks enthusiasm, curbs procrastination and self doubt.

Low levels of dopamine is associated with these issues. Set goals, achieve them, even if they are micro goals. There's something truly beneficial about ticking off goals. Some ways to naturally boost dopamine are adding turmeric to your diet, using herbs like ginkgo biloba, getting natural sunlight and drinking green tea.

It's worth getting a good understanding of how you can generally increase brain health. When things are not going so well in the body, the body will give us small signs. We tend to put down these signs to ageing or tiredness. But anytime you're given a sign, you should be paying more attention. Especially, when it's mental. Think of a time you needed an answer, you knew it but you could not recall it, now imagine if you could recall it and recall it fast. How beneficial would that be day to day? Especially, whilst working in high pressure jobs.

Our brains use up to 20% of our energy, it's our most energy-consuming organ. For that reason we need to ensure that what we consume is good energy and that we fuel our brains right.

Below are some symptoms of reduced brain health that you need to be mindful of:

1. Forgetfulness (especially short-term memory)
2. Cravings
3. Inability to focus
4. Low energy
5. Moodiness / anger
6. Lack of good sleep

My eyes opened after reading a book called Head Strong by Dave Asprey, a book I highly recommend. He speaks about how to supercharge the brain. Some key takeaways from the book that I recommend to my coaching clients are as follows.

TAKE MORE BRAIN HERBS

We have already discussed herbs like Cacao but there are other herbs that are beneficial like Ginseng Panax, Ginkgo Biloba and Damiana. These herbs can be a good alternative to your daily tea whilst at work. Allowing you to take a moment to recharge yourself and supercharge the brain. Feel good, do good, be rewarded and climb the corporate ladder.

JUNK LIGHT CONSUMPTION

A study into screen time revealed office workers spend an average of six and a half hours a day sitting at their computer or laptop.

During this time our bodies are consuming a ridiculous amount of junk light. Recent studies have shown that over-exposure to artificial light at the wrong time of day can have negative effects on your sleep and, in turn, your mental and physical performance during the day. Light is an important cue to the body as to when to go to sleep or when to wake up.Additionally, it signals when it's time to wind down. Our bodies struggle with high levels of junk light.

LEDs and fluorescents are emitting nearly 5 times the blue light we are equipped to handle.

The junk light can impact sleep, make you feel fatigued and also impact your sleep quality. I've installed f.lux on both my PC and laptop, and tend to use night shift mode on my iPhone. My sleep quality and productivity have increased since. I implore you to do this now then watch your health and productivity spike. Additionally, you won't mind working on your computer for longer.

BRAIN DIET

The brain needs good fuel to maintain focus and concentration throughout the day. Have you seen the movie limitless? In case you haven't seen the movie, Eddie Morra's life is changed when he is given a drug that produces enhanced mental acuity. Allowing him to unlock up to 100% use of his brain. Although there is no pill that can do that now, there is a diet that can help at least give you the best possible results. That is the brain diet. Foods that are beneficial for the brain include healthy fats, minimal sugar, brain fruits and leafy green vegetables.

Here is a table of foods recommended to boost the brain:

Veggies	spinach, callaloo, kale, red peppers, squash, carrots and broccoli
Nuts	cashew nuts, almonds, walnuts and brazil nuts
Fruits	blueberries, strawberries, bananas, goji berry, bilberries and avocados
Grains	quinoa, amaranth and lentils such as brown and green lentils
Oils	avocado oil, extra virgin olive oil, pumpkin seed oil, black seed oil and MCT oil

Avoid processed foods and foods high in sugar. Additionally, avoid inflammatory fats as they are brain limiting foods. I'd recommend getting a smoothie maker, either keeping it in the office or at home, as it's a fast way to get a nutrient boost to the day.

BRAIN LIMITING FOODS

There are foods that as soon as you consume them you notice a shift in your energy and focus. Have you ever had a big meal and expected to feel energetic and full of life? But instead you feel tired or sleepy. You don't want this to happen at 1pm straight after lunch. Brain limiting foods can have that effect.

The main culprits are sugar and sugary drinks. Sugary drinks include fruit juice, sodas, energy drinks and sports drinks. When you turn over the drink and see the nutrient table, it's not always easy to put the sugar content into perspective. Think of it this way, 4 grams of sugar is equivalent to 1 cube or 1 teaspoon of sugar. A can of Coke contains 39 grams of sugar. That's almost 10 cubes of sugar or 10 teaspoons.

Sugar in the body wreaks havoc, especially as you're trying to climb the corporate ladder. The brain's main fuel is glucose but excess glucose in the brain impairs cognitive skills resulting in slowed cognitive function in addition to deficits in memory and attention.

Also, sugar can make you crave more sugar and become hungry leading to more sugar cravings and weight gain. A few people I've told about how sugar can disrupt the brain and cause havoc in the body, found solace in the fact they can still drink diet drinks. Now, the sad news, many diet products are even worse for the body and brain than the original because of the artificial sweeteners used.

The most common sweetener used in diet and sugar free products is Aspartame. There is a very long list of potential ailments that aspartame apparently causes; from cancer to birth defects. In terms of being fully optimised for the workplace, aspartame can potentially disrupt the product of neurotransmitters, increase irritability, rates of depression and reduce cognitive function, especially memory. Some studies suggest it does and some suggest it doesn't but there is no such thing as something for nothing. A sweetener with no sugar should be used with caution. It's worth being mindful of gluten, as gluten can trigger inflammation in the body, affect your mitochondria and limit the production of tryptophan, an amino acid that is the precursor to serotonin.

Did you know that up to 97% of women and 68% of men report experiencing some sort of food craving, the most common craving is a craving for sugar.

Many sugar cravings stem from a blood sugar imbalance. When we consume a sugary food, the blood sugar spikes and the body releases insulin to bring the blood sugar back to a normal level. But the insulin may bring your blood sugar level to a level lower than normal which in turn makes your body crave foods (sugar) that raise the blood sugar level and raise your energy.

Foods that fight cravings include fruits such as berries, mangos, sweet potatoes, and herbs like bilberry tea.

ENERGY

Our energy during winter tends to drop, below are a few tips to help you keep your energy up and boost productivity at work whilst others are feeling the energy dip.

There are 3 main reasons why you're feeling tired, these are:

- Diet
- Exercise
- Sleep

These reasons is especially important for the brain in winter. Heres how shorter days impact your brain:

- **Metabolism**. Research shows that as the days get shorter and colder we may have an ingrained behaviour to eat more than usual to store energy.
- **Energy**. Your body produces a hormone called melatonin in darkness — typically at bedtime. Melatonin impacts sleep patterns and energy levels.
- **Attention**. Alertness and cognitive function decrease due to changes in your hypothalamus, the part of your brain responsible for sleep and circadian rhythm.
- **Mood**. Neurotransmitters serotonin and dopamine decrease, which can contribute to depression.

To help you stay optimal, here are key nutrients to ensure that you're getting are during winter:

- Iron
- Potassium
- Vitamin B12
- Zinc
- Magnesium

Sea moss and Dulse seaweed (also a good source of iodine & Vitamin B12) are great sources of these nutrients, sea moss has 92 of the 102 minerals the body is made from.

It's also possible that your thyroid gland is a reason you're feeling tired and sluggish. A key nutrient needed for optimal thyroid function is iodine. The thyroid gland also controls your metabolism. Thus looking after your thyroid can help you keep the fat off through the winter.

Lastly, during the winter there is less sun to get your Vitamin D3 from, you need a backup plan. Perhaps it's time to grab fat soluble Vitamin D3 supplement as 29 per cent of UK adults are vitamin D deficient between January and March. Vitamin D is vital for making our muscles work efficiently and boosting energy levels. Helping you stay energised at work.

SUGAR & FAT

When considering whether you want to have that extra slice of cake or maybe, if you should get a cookie with your coffee from Pret, consider these 4 ways sugar can make you fat. Then make an informed decision.

1 - Eating foods high in sugar can increase hunger, promoting hormone ghrelin and reduce appetite surprising hormone peptide YY, potentially making you eat more.

2 - Sugar is addictive. Once sugar is consumed, dopamine is released, and you can feel satisfied but once the insulin response clears the blood of sugar, you can become hungry again but this hunger experience is typically a craving for more sugar

3 - High sugar foods will lead to high blood sugar, which triggers the release of insulin. When insulin levels are high, the body doesn't use fat stores for fuel, it uses the glucose in the blood. Making it harder to burn the fat stores if constant.

4 - Excess blood sugar must be stored somehow. Insulin will push the sugar into cells to be used as energy but if it's not used, it can be stored inside the fat cells.

Remember balance is key. Empty calories (a food that has no or limited nutritional value, like cakes and fizzy drinks) can be a treat but being aware of the impact allows you to plan your daily or weekly intake according to your goals.

EXERCISE

Exercise is a key chapter for all of those looking to climb the corporate ladder effectively. The high performers of the world like Elon Musk, Mark Cuban and Richard Branson all incorporate exercise as part of their routine. Richard Branson claims that exercise adds 4 hours of productivity to his day. That's 4 hours more than your competitors for the promotion. Exercise impacts almost every area of your life.

Exercise will help with brain fog, stress, mood, productivity, memory, confidence, sharpness and your general health, meaning you take fewer sick days. All of which are valuable in the workplace. From as little as 30 minutes a day you can experience benefits that propel your career and make you work more efficiently.

There are many other benefits of exercise, but I know time can be an issue in most offices. That's why I am adding a workout plan that you can do anywhere; in the office during lunch time or at home with minimal equipment. If you add jogging or walking to the plan, you will have all the exercise you need to boost your capabilities at work.

Head to www.paulotote.com/exercise for a workout routine you can do anywhere, including your office. It's a video routine and I will do the workout with you.

Another benefit of exercise is its effect on mental health. One study found that lifting weights (resistance training) reduces the symptoms of anxiety, Another found that lifting weights can help ease and even prevent depression". This a big reason to start exercising today.

There are other mental health benefits of exercise too. It's been noted that exercise can help create changes such as the formation of new brain cells, stronger connections between those cells, as well as the creation of new blood vessels, which provide your brain with oxygen and essential nutrients.

Exercise is key to being the best version of you and thus ramping up productivity in the workplace. Start today with just 20 minutes.

A WINNER'S DIET

The diet of winners is the diet I eat and one that has worked amazingly for me. But finding the balance that works for you is something that you have to figure out for yourself. I eat a strict plant-based diet and it has worked wonders for my life from my physique to mental strength to my mood. Understanding the key principles of a plant-based diet allows you to knit pick some parts of it that can add value for your life and wellbeing, especially in the workplace.

The basis of a plant-based diet is eating wholefoods, unprocessed and natural. A vegan diet on the other hand can be a plant-based diet but due to its focus on animals, a lot of vegans skip the wholefood element and focus on just cutting meat products from their lifestyle.

This means that they might not always have the best healthy diet as that's not their focus.. I've been coaching for years and those who I have recommended the following foods to see the benefits, even by adding just one of the main ingredients to their diet. The foundation foods are grains, vegetables, beans, legumes, fruits, herbs and nuts.

Wholegrains include quinoa, amaranth, spelt, oats and brown rice. I personally try to avoid gluten, so I avoid eating whole wheat.

 I eat legumes such as beans, lentils and chickpeas. These are high in nutrients and protein to help the body heal and feel revitalised. I also have a book on nutrients, it breaks down all the nutrients the body requires and where I get them from a plant-based diet, it's available on Amazon.

In terms of herbs, I have a lot of videos on Youtube on herbs and I have a book on herbs as previously mentioned, the book will help you understand herbs that supercharge the mind and body.

Nuts, I eat all nuts, but I eat cashew nuts most regularly. Other foods I eat are yams, plantains, sweet potatoes and mushrooms. Mushrooms are a great source of Vitamin D2.

Adding any of these to your diet can improve your life in 2 weeks and you will see a noticeable change at work. Whether you want to go full plant-based or just add elements of a healthy diet to your life, little changes have big impact and you will see the results.

In terms of herbs, I have a lot of videos on Youtube on herbs and I have a book on herbs as previously mentioned, the book will help you understand herbs that supercharge the mind and body.

Nuts, I eat all nuts, but I eat cashew nuts most regularly. Other foods I eat are yams, plantains, sweet potatoes and mushrooms. Mushrooms are a great source of Vitamin D2.

Adding any of these to your diet can improve your life in 2 weeks and you will see a noticeable change at work. Whether you want to go full plant-based or just add elements of a healthy diet to your life, little changes have big impact and you will see the results.

FIGHTING CRAVINGS

The road to health is littered with temptations, the biggest temptations are cravings. Especially during that time of the month for women. The most common cravings are for sugar, salt and cheese. Mastering cravings can literally change your life and help you create sustainable habits. But you need to plan for how you will respond to cravings.

Some research shows that some food cravings are your body's natural, instinctive way of letting you know you that you need more of an important nutrient.

Cheese can be associated with calcium and Vitamin B12 deficiency, for example. It's worth researching the underlying reason why you're craving a food. I recommend a blood test to some clients.

On a simplistic level, you can try:

- Bilberry for sugar cravings
- Pumpkin / sesame seeds (and other seeds) for salt cravings
- Cacao for chocolate cravings

I would recommend Bilberry, knowing it worked for me as I used to have a massive sweet tooth.

You enjoy foods so much more when you're not a slave to them. We can also have an emotional attachment to foods based on memories, for example, people can associate sweets with good memories, as there tends to be sweet things like cake whenever there is a celebration. For example, your birthdays growing up. Introspection can help you finally beat your cravings once and for all. So, you can think more about the work in front of you and less about the donut in the fridge.

WORK DESK PRACTICAL TIPS

The workstation is crucial to having an unfair advantage. Some use their desk to benefit their career, others choose to use it to their demise. I'd like to give you a few tips on how to use the work desk to your advantage. Firstly, do you have a snack drawer?

Stocking your snack drawer with fresh fruits, nuts and other healthy snacks can help boost your brain power throughout the day.

There will be times where you have been working for three hour straight and you need something to give you that extra energy and concentration boost.

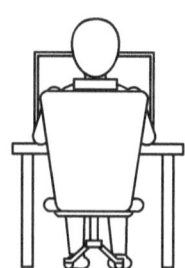

Being able to quickly get some strawberries and take your mind off things may allow you to get the real fuel you need. Additionally, this will help you avoid going to the shop hungry, and we all know what happens when we do that.

Staying more productive through the day can allow you to seamlessly do more and think more creative through the day. Especially in roles, such as finance and law, where attention to detail can make or break your career.

Key fruits to have in your drawer:

- Blueberry
- Cashew nuts
- Pumpkin seeds
- Walnuts
- Oranges
- Green tea
- Lemongrass
- Cherry
- Banana
- Almond
- Pomegranate
- Avocados
- Strawberries
- Blackberries
- Grapes
- Gingko tea
- Water
- Raspberry

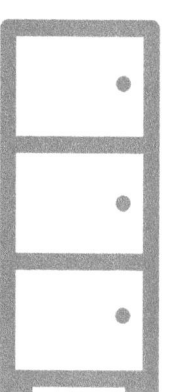

You can keep some hummus with some turmeric in the fridge and use it as a dip, that's the brain boost you need at any time.

These foods will stop cravings, help you lose weight and give you that boost when you need it. Restock your deck once a week and see your productivity sky rocket.

Other things you can do is have a desk plant, psychologists have found that, as well as oxygenating the air, bringing some flora into the workplace can improve employee satisfaction and can increase productivity by up to 15%.

SLEEP

Sleep is the last chapter to supercharging your career at work. Most of us do not get enough sleep and it impacts us in ways we may not be aware of. Sleep affects productivity, creativity, emotional balance, brain and heart health, immune system, vitality, and even your weight. Some people struggling to lose weight have no idea that the reason they can't shift fat from their stomach area is due to a lack of sleep

The average adult needs between 7-9 hours of sleep, in some situations 6-11 may be appropriate but even minimal sleep loss can take a substantial toll on your mood, energy, mental sharpness, and ability to handle stress.

EPILOGUE

I really hope this book has helped you understand how to improve your health and use it to achieve your career goals.

A bit about me, I am a entrepreneur, coach and wellness expert with over 10 years experience. As I certified herbalist & nutritionist I share practical ideas to help people improve their day to day lives. Teaching preventative methods online through content. I've authored 3 other books such as Complete Herb List Guide For Beginners and Complete Nutrient Guide For Beginners.

If you would like to invite me to your workplace to give a session or if you received a promotion in part due to this book, drop me a note to paul@paulotote.com

Special thanks to Marian Enume for helping with editing and proofreading.

www.ingramcontent.com/pod-product-compliance
Lightning Source LLC
Chambersburg PA
CBHW070854220526
45466CB00005B/2000